The Trouble Ball

Other Books by Martín Espada

POETRY

Soldados en el Jardín
La Tumba de Buenaventura Roig
Crucifixion in the Plaza de Armas
The Republic of Poetry
Alabanza: New and Selected Poems 1982–2002
A Mayan Astronomer in Hell's Kitchen
Imagine the Angels of Bread
City of Coughing and Dead Radiators
Rebellion Is the Circle of a Lover's Hands
Trumpets from the Islands of Their Eviction
The Immigrant Iceboy's Bolero

AS TRANSLATOR

*The Blood That Keeps Singing: Selected Poems of
    Clemente Soto Vélez* (with Camilo Pérez-Bustillo)

AS EDITOR

El Coro: A Chorus of Latino and Latina Poetry
*Poetry Like Bread: Poets of the Political Imagination
    from Curbstone Press*

ESSAYS

Auf der Suche nach La Revolución
The Lover of a Subversive Is Also a Subversive
Zapata's Disciple

AUDIOBOOK

Now the Dead Will Dance the Mambo

The
TROUBLE BALL

POEMS

Martín Espada

W. W. Norton & Company
New York · London

Excerpt from *Walking Words* by Eduardo Galeano, translated by Mark Fried.
Copyright © 1993 by Eduardo Galeano. Translation copyright © 1995 by Mark
Fried. Used by permission of the author and W. W. Norton & Company, Inc.

For information about permission to reproduce selections from this
book, write to Permissions, W. W. Norton & Company, Inc.,
500 Fifth Avenue, New York, NY 10110

For information about special discounts for bulk purchases, please contact
W. W. Norton Special Sales at specialsales@wwnorton.com or 800-233-4830

Manufacturing by Courier Westford
Book design by Charlotte Staub
Production manager: Devon Zahn

Library of Congress Cataloging-in-Publication Data

Espada, Martín, date.
The trouble ball : poems / Martín Espada. — 1st ed.
       p. cm.
ISBN 978-0-393-08003-2 (hardcover)
I. Title.
PS3555.S53T68 2011
811'.54—dc22

                                        2010041046

ISBN 978-0-393-34356-4 pbk.

W. W. Norton & Company, Inc.
500 Fifth Avenue, New York, N.Y. 10110
www.wwnorton.com

W. W. Norton & Company Ltd.
Castle House, 75/76 Wells Street, London W1T 3QT

2 3 4 5 6 7 8 9 0

Dedicated to the memory of

Alexander "Sandy" Taylor (1931–2007)

Abe Osheroff (1915–2008)

Adrian Mitchell (1932–2008)

Howard Zinn (1922–2010)

and Isabel

CONTENTS

Part One: THE TROUBLE BALL

Part Two: BLASPHEMY

ACKNOWLEDGMENTS

These poems have appeared or will appear in the following publications, to whose editors grateful acknowledgment is made:

Adrian: Scotland Celebrates Adrian Mitchell (Markings Publications): "Epiphany"

Black Renaissance Noire: "The Trouble Ball"

The Bloomsbury Review: "Litany at the Tomb of Frederick Douglass," "Visions of the Chapel Ceiling in Guadalajara"

The Café Review: "The Swimming Pool at Villa Grimaldi"

Cutthroat (online): "Isabel's Corrido"

Event: "Isabel's Corrido," "The Hole in the Bathroom Ceiling," "My Heart Kicked Like a Mouse in a Paper Bag"

Green Mountains Review: "The Buried Book of Jorge Montealegre," "His Hands Have Learned What Cannot Be Taught," "How to Read Ezra Pound," "The Rowboat"

Guernica (online): "People Like Us Are Dangerous"

Hanging Loose: "Blessed Be the Truth-Tellers"

La Bloga (online): "Isabel's Corrido"

Markings: "The Rowboat"

The Massachusetts Review: "The Day We Buried You in the Park"

MELUS: "A Traveling Salesman in the Gardens of Paradise," "Blasphemy," "Instructions on the Disposal of My Remains," "Mr. and Mrs. Rodríguez Have Been Deported, Leaving Six Children Behind with the Neighbors"

Naked Punch: "Epiphany"

New Humanist: "The *Playboy* Calendar and the *Rubáiyát* of Omar Khayyám," "Isabel's Corrido"

Open Letters Monthly (online): "The Swimming Pool at Villa Grimaldi"

Penniless Press (online): "Walking"

Poetry Daily: "Blessed Be the Truth-Tellers"

The Progressive: "Like a Word That Somersaults Through the Air," "The *Playboy* Calendar and the *Rubáiyát* of Omar Khayyám," "Walking"

Review: Literature and the Arts of the Americas: "The Spider and the Angel," "Visions of the Chapel Ceiling in Guadalajara"

Rosebud: "The Swimming Pool at Villa Grimaldi"

So Much Things to Say (Peepal Tree Press/Akashic Books): "The Swimming Pool at Villa Grimaldi"

Southword (online): "A Traveling Salesman in the Gardens of Paradise," "The Swimming Pool at Villa Grimaldi," "His Hands Have Learned What Cannot Be Taught"

Many thanks to the following individuals and organizations: to Ed Carvalho, for the Espada Journal; to Denise Chávez, for the Border Book Festival; to Andy Croft, for Smokestack Books and the Radical Poets Tour; to Frank and Marilyn Espada, my parents, for the stories; to Katherine and Klemente Gilbert-Espada, my wife and son, for their patience; to Frances Goldin, for her zealous representation; to Rachel Eliza Griffiths, for the photograph on the Brooklyn Bridge; to Arturo Madrid, for his support; to John Murillo, for his tattoo; to César Salgado, for all his work on my behalf as editor, essayist, and translator; to Oscar Sarmiento, for his translations, his help with the Jorge Montealegre poem and the journey to Villa Grimaldi; to Steve Stern, for his invaluable assistance with the Villa Grimaldi poem; to Fish Vargas and Rich Villar, for the Acentos workshop and a memorable visit to White Castle; and to the National Hispanic Cultural Center, for their Literary Award.

Part One

The

TROUBLE BALL

The Trouble Ball

for my father, Frank Espada

In 1941, my father saw his first big league ballgame at Ebbets Field
in Brooklyn: the Dodgers and the Cardinals. My father took his father's hand.
When the umpires lumbered on the field, the band in the stands
with a bass drum and trombone struck up a chorus of *Three Blind Mice.*
The peanut vendor shook a cowbell and hollered. The home team
raced across the diamond, and thirty thousand people shouted
all at once, as if an army of liberation rolled down Bedford Avenue.
My father shouted, too. He wanted to see The Trouble Ball.

On my father's island, there were hurricanes and tuberculosis, dissidents in jail
and baseball. The loudspeakers boomed: *Satchel Paige pitching for the Brujos
of Guayama.* From the Negro Leagues he brought the gifts of Baltasar the King;
from a bench on the plaza he told the secrets of a thousand pitches: The Trouble Ball,
The Triple Curve, The Bat Dodger, The Midnight Creeper, The Slow Gin Fizz,
The Thoughtful Stuff. Pancho Coímbre hit rainmakers for the Leones of Ponce;
Satchel sat the outfielders in the grass to play poker, windmilled three pitches
to the plate, and Pancho spun around three times. He couldn't hit The Trouble Ball.

At Ebbets Field, the first pitch echoed in the mitt of Mickey Owen,
the catcher for the Dodgers who never let the ball escape his glove.
A boy off the boat, my father shelled peanuts, waiting for Satchel Paige
to steer his gold Cadillac from the bullpen to the mound, just as he would
navigate the streets of Guayama. Yet Satchel never tipped his cap that day.
¿Dónde están los negros? asked the boy. *Where are the Negro players?*
No los dejan, his father softly said. *They don't let them play here.*
Mickey Owen would never have to dive for The Trouble Ball.

It was then that the only brown boy at Ebbets Field felt himself
levitate above the grandstand and the diamond, another banner
at the ballgame. From up high he could see that everyone was white,
and their whiteness was impossible, like snow in Puerto Rico,
and just as silent, so he could not hear the cowbell, or the trombone,
or the Dodger fans howling with glee at the bases-loaded double.
He understood why his father whispered in Spanish: everybody
in the stands might overhear the secret of The Trouble Ball.

At Ebbets Field in 1941, the Dodgers met the Yankees in the World Series.
Mickey Owen dropped the third strike with two outs in the ninth inning
of Game Four, flailing like a lobster in the grip of a laughing fisherman,
and the Yankees stamped their spikes across the plate to win. Brooklyn,
the borough of churches, prayed for his fumbling soul. This was the reason
statues of the Virgin leaked tears and the fathers of Brooklyn drank,
not the banishment of Satchel Paige to doubleheaders in Bismarck,
North Dakota. There were no rosaries or boilermakers for The Trouble Ball.

My father would return to baseball on 108th Street. He pitched for the Crusaders,
kicking high like Satchel, riding the team bus painted with four-leaf clovers, seasick
all the way to Hackensack or the Brooklyn Parade Grounds. One day he jammed
his wrist sliding into second, threw three more innings anyway, and never pitched again.
He would return to Ebbets Field to court my mother. The same year they were married
a waiter refused to serve them, a mixed couple sitting all night in the corner,
till my father hoisted him by his lapels and the waiter's feet dangled in the air,
a puppet and his furious puppeteer. My father was familiar with The Trouble Ball.

I was born in Brooklyn in 1957, when the Dodgers packed their duffle bags
and left the city. A wrecking ball swung an uppercut into the face
of Ebbets Field. I heard the stories: how my mother, lost in the circles

and diamonds of her scorecard, never saw Jackie Robinson accelerate
down the line to steal home. I wore my father's glove until the day
I laid it down to lap the water from the fountain in the park. By the time
I raised my head, it was gone like Ebbets Field. I walked slowly home.
I had to tell my father I would never learn to catch The Trouble Ball.

There was a sign below the scoreboard at Ebbets Field: *Abe Stark, Brooklyn's
Leading Clothier. Hit Sign, Win Suit.* Some people see that sign in dreams.
They speak of ballparks as cathedrals, frame the pennants from the game
where it began, Dodger blue and Cardinal red, and gaze upon the wall.
My father, who remembers everything, remembers nothing of that dazzling day
but this: *¿Dónde están los negros? No los dejan.* His hair is white, and still
the words are there, like the ghostly imprint of stitches on the forehead
from a pitch that got away. It is forever 1941. It was The Trouble Ball.

Blessed Be the Truth-Tellers

for Jack Agüeros

In the projects of Brooklyn, everyone lied.
My mother used to say:
If somebody starts a fight,
just walk away.
Then somebody would smack
the back of my head |
and dance around me in a circle, laughing.

When I was twelve, pus bubbled
on my tonsils, and everyone said:
After the operation, you can have
all the ice cream you want.
I bragged about the deal;
no longer would I chase the ice-cream truck
down the street, panting at the bells
to catch Johnny the ice-cream man,
who allegedly sold heroin the color of vanilla
from the same window.

Then Jack the Truth-Teller visited the projects,
Jack who herded real camels and sheep
through the snow of East Harlem every Three Kings' Day,
Jack who wrote sonnets of the jail cell
and the racetrack and the boxing ring,
Jack who crossed his arms in a hunger strike
until the mayor hired more Puerto Ricans.

And Jack said:
You gonna get your tonsils out?
Ay bendito cuchifrito Puerto Rico.
That's gonna hurt.

I was etherized,
then woke up on the ward
heaving black water onto white sheets.
A man poking through his hospital gown
leaned over me and sneered,
You think you got it tough? Look at this!
and showed me the cauliflower tumor
behind his ear. I heaved up black water again.

The ice cream burned.
Vanilla was a snowball spiked with bits of glass.
My throat was red as a tunnel on fire
after the head-on collision of two gasoline trucks.

This is how I learned to trust
the poets and shepherds of East Harlem.
Blessed be the Truth-Tellers,
for they shall have all the ice cream they want.

The Spider and the Angel

Day camp in the summer of 1968:
The counselors steered us to the roof
of a school building in Brooklyn,
slapped down soggy mattresses
and told us to wrestle.

A boy from Puerto Rico,
crazy as a spider in the bathroom sink,
heard my crippled Spanish
and decided I was not the Puerto Rican
that I claimed to be. With his thumbs
he tried to pop my eyeballs from their sockets.
The counselors smoked and nodded.

The next day they matched me with Angel.
I swung my elbow back into his mouth
and he bled like a martyr.
If he could have flown home to the island
by leaping from that rooftop,
he would have spread his arms and jumped.

The spider-boy realized then
that I was Puerto Rican after all.
He stayed close to me that summer,
promising to jab his thumbs into the eyes
of anyone who disrespected me.

I never did aim my finger at the enemy
who should be blinded next.
I was satisfied. We were Puerto Ricans,
wrestling for the approval of our keepers,
inches from rolling off the roof.

People Like Us Are Dangerous

In Brooklyn days, I wanted to be Carlos Ortiz, lightweight champion
of the world from Ponce, Puerto Rico. I gazed at the radiance
of the black and white television till it spoke to me in tongues,
a boy spellbound by the grainy spirits who stalked each other in the ring.

I wanted to be Carlos Ortiz when twenty thousand people
at Shea Stadium chanted his name. For fifteen rounds the jazz
percussion of his punches beat the sweat from Ismael Laguna,
El Tigre de Santa Isabel, who lurched off the ropes,
backpedaled and swallowed blood till the last bell.

I wanted to crouch and dip into the arc of my uppercut
like Carlos Ortiz on the cover of *The Ring* magazine,
where they called him *a pugilist with clever hands.*
I wanted to be a pugilist with clever hands. My father
bought me boxing gloves and I reddened my brother's face.
I shadowboxed all the way down the hall.

I wanted something from the clever hand of Carlos Ortiz.
My mother and my father's sister, dressed for the dance floor
at the Club Tropicoro, tracked the champ to the men's room
and offered him a cocktail napkin to sign for me.
He grinned like the general of a people's army
greeting the crowd from a balcony at the presidential palace.

I told everyone in the streets of Brooklyn I wanted to be
a Puerto Rican fighter like Carlos Ortiz. Every day I sparred

in the schoolyard until a boy I did not know waved his hands
in a circle, mesmerizing as a hypnotist, then kicked me
with his hard-soled shoe in a place I could not bring myself to name.
The blood crusted between my legs. I threw away my underwear.

Years later, I met Carlos Ortiz stirring milk into his coffee
at a McDonald's off the New York Thruway.
The black curls on his forehead had disappeared, along
with the Club Tropicoro and the eighty thousand dollars
he counted out in cash to build his palace of trumpets in the Bronx.

Year by year, the whiskey and the beer wore away the levees
of his brain till he walked like a man underwater. One night
at Madison Square Garden, unable to move his arms or legs,
he stared at the canvas and quit on his stool. Carlos Ortiz drove
a cab on graveyard shift to keep away from all the bars on the avenue,
far from the backslappers who wanted to buy the champ a drink.

Carlos Ortiz is sober now. He thinks of Ismael Laguna, who cannot
pry open his hands, selling souvenir newspapers with headlines about
El Tigre de Santa Isabel. Carlos Ortiz says: *People like us are dangerous.*

A Traveling Salesman in the Gardens of Paradise

for Gisela Conn

Jardines del Paraíso: The Gardens of Paradise,
or so we'd say, staring into our coffee, whenever
we translated the name of the public housing projects
where my grandmother smoked on the porch,
watching the trade in dollars and drugs
swiftly move from hand to hand
in Río Piedras, Puerto Rico.

One night a visitor called her name
through the shutters of the window,
going door to door with something to sell:
a car battery in his hands, offered with the pride
of a diver showing off a treasure chest
salvaged from the bottom of the sea.

He was a traveling salesman in the Gardens of Paradise.
I was a traveling salesman once, selling encyclopedias
door to door, buying only the cheapest leads
from people who wrote: *I want to win a free encyclopedia.*
Don't send me a salesman. Door after door slapped shut.
I quit one day, when the cops spotted me reading maps
spread across the steering wheel, and held me for hours
in the parking lot, suspected of stealing my own car.
The little cop wore sunglasses in the rain, asking repeatedly
if I was wanted by the police. *I don't know*, I said. *Do you want me?*

Let him in, I proclaimed that night in the Gardens of Paradise.
We broke the reverie of arroz con pollo steaming on the fork.
Cousin Gisela greeted the salesman with his offering,
then had a vision brilliant as the halo of Jesus on the wall:
her car in the parking lot with the hood propped up
and the battery missing. *Did you get that from my car?*
asked Gisela, like a teacher aggravated by another theft
of cookies from her desk. *You put that back right now.*
With apologies and a bow, he did.

He was a tecato, Gisela said, another junkie with a face
from the neighborhood. The next day my grandmother,
who believed that even junkies have a place in Paradise,
called to the same tecato through the window,
handed him her last five dollars,
and sent him to the store for cigarettes.

There would be buying and selling
that night in the Gardens of Paradise,
and witnesses who would never testify
chain-smoking on the porch.

My Heart Kicked Like a Mouse
in a Paper Bag

I was on the cleaning crew for two dollars an hour,
wheeling a trash cart through the aisles at Sears,
panning for cigarettes in the sand of ashtrays, fumbling
fluorescent tubes that exploded when they hit the floor.
I once removed the perfect turd from a urinal, fastidiously
as an Egyptologist handling the scat of a pharaoh.

Some of the janitor's boys were Black men with white hair;
the rest wore badges with missing letters in Spanish.
We heard four bells and galloped across the store.
The janitor sat all day in the boiler room
reading Asian mail-order bride magazines.

I was the boy who swam in trash. I dumped the carts
into the compacter we dubbed the Crusher, then
leaped on the pile to pack it down. Sometimes,
I'd jump on the garbage and burst through
like a skater too heavy for the ice on a frozen lake.
Once a trashman who did not see me pressed the button,
and the walls of the Crusher began to grind. I yelled
and the grinding stopped. The janitor never knew;
he was masturbating in the boiler room.

A stock boy handed me a paper bag one night
as if it were the lunch he forgot to eat, and punched out.
The bag was alive. There was a mouse inside, kicking,
caught sniffing around the Crusher. Bewildered boy

that I was, I called security, department store cops
who loitered at the loading dock, breath hot
from smoking, hunting shoplifters and telling lies
about the war. One of them said: *Where's the mouse?*

When he clapped the bag in his hands it popped, and the pop
made me flinch, and the flinch made him slam the bag again,
till the strawberry stain told me the interrogation was over.
He flipped the bleeding sack at me, and walked away.
My heart kicked like a mouse in a paper bag.

Today I stomp on the trash behind the shed, packing it down for the barrels
I steer into the road. Gathering the cigarettes I do not smoke, that float
in the coffee I do not drink, satisfies the cleaning crew in me.
I hear the four bells like a fighter with the same headache for forty years.
Sometimes I search the garbage with a flashlight for an unpaid bill,
a bottle of pills, a lost letter, the perfect mouse to liberate.

The Hole in the Bathroom Ceiling

I've seen holes in the ceiling:
in the kitchen ceiling, dripping percussive
rain into saucepans on the table;
in the living room ceiling, leaking
drops that burst between the eyes
of a visitor sitting on the couch;
in the bedroom ceiling, drizzling the spittle
onto the pillow that freezes overnight
and sticks to my head in the morning.

There is a hole in the bathroom ceiling bigger than my head.
God put the hole in the bathroom ceiling right over the toilet.
The plastic tacked over the hole flaps open, and a bounty
cascades from the heavens: the drywall soaked and crumbling
like a donut forgotten in a cup of coffee; the spiders swimming
to freedom that paddle happily, then panic and drown;
the mold that floats down into my lungs, where it will
strangle me in my sleep; the incontinence of rusted pipes
spraying in every direction. Everything tumbles
into the toilet, lid up, eager as the mouth
of a trained dolphin begging for fish at the aquarium.

For the hole right over the toilet, I fold my hands
and give thanks to God. I do not ruin saucepans
catching the rain, or befoul towels pushing them across
the floor with my feet, or fill pails that also leak.
Sometimes I must slam the plunger into the toilet,

eyes bulging with the fury of a sea captain harpooning
his nemesis the whale. Sometimes I open an umbrella
when I squat on the toilet. Sometimes I forget
till something cold and wet slaps the back of my neck.

Once a landlord tried to hand me an eviction notice. I chased him
back to his Toyota and kicked in the driver's side door, a moose
enraged by the economy car that dared to bruise his knees.
The bank owns the house and the hole in the bathroom ceiling;
there is nowhere left to kick. Think of all the holes
in all the ceilings everywhere, and thank God.

His Hands Have Learned
What Cannot Be Taught

My wife has had another seizure,
the kind where she seems to be dead,
her eyes open and unseeing,
like jellyfish dangling
in the ocean at midnight.

My son, not yet seventeen,
leans across the table
and shuts her eyelids
with the V of his fingers.

When she wakes,
she will not know why she dropped her coffee.
She will not know his name, or mine, at first.
She will not know that he closed her eyes.
I will know that his hands have learned
what cannot be taught, that now
I can leave the table.

The Poet's Son Watches His Father Leave for Another Gig

Once again
you're choosing
between dignity
and Christmas

Isabel's Corrido

Para Isabel

Francisca said: *Marry my sister so she can stay in the country.*
I had nothing else to do. I was twenty-three and always cold, skidding
in cigarette-coupon boots from lamppost to lamppost through January
in Wisconsin. Francisca and Isabel washed bed sheets at the hotel,
sweating in the humidity of the laundry room, conspiring in Spanish.

I met her the next day. Isabel was nineteen, from a village where the elders
spoke the language of the Aztecs. She would smile whenever the ice pellets
of English clattered around her head. When the justice of the peace said
You may kiss the bride, our lips brushed for the first and only time.
The borrowed ring was too small, jammed into my knuckle.
There were snapshots of the wedding and champagne in plastic cups.

Francisca said: *The snapshots will be proof for Immigration.*
We heard rumors of the interview: they would ask me the color
of her underwear. They would ask her who rode on top.
We invented answers and rehearsed our lines. We flipped through
Immigration forms at the kitchen table the way other couples
shuffled cards for gin rummy. After every hand, I'd deal again.

Isabel would say: *Quiero ver las fotos.* She wanted to see the pictures
of a wedding that happened but did not happen, her face inexplicably
happy, me hoisting a green bottle, dizzy after half a cup of champagne.

Francisca said: *She can sing corridos,* songs of love and revolution
from the land of Zapata. All night Isabel sang corridos in a barroom

where no one understood a word. I was the bouncer and her husband,
so I hushed the squabbling drunks, who blinked like tortoises in the sun.

Her boyfriend and his beer cans never understood why she married me.
Once he kicked the front door down, and the blast shook the house
as if a hand grenade detonated in the hallway. When the cops arrived,
I was the translator, watching the sergeant watching her, the inscrutable
squaw from every Western he had ever seen, bare feet and long black hair.

We lived behind a broken door. We lived in a city hidden from the city.
When her headaches began, no one called a doctor. When she disappeared
for days, no one called the police. When we rehearsed the questions
for Immigration, Isabel would squint and smile. *Quiero ver las fotos*,
she would say. The interview was canceled, like a play on opening night
shut down when the actors are too drunk to take the stage. After she left,
I found her crayon drawing of a bluebird tacked to the bedroom wall.

I left too, and did not think of Isabel again until the night Francisca called to say:
Your wife is dead. Something was growing in her brain. I imagined my wife
who was not my wife, who never slept beside me, sleeping in the ground,
wondered if my name was carved into the cross above her head, no epitaph
and no corrido, another ghost in a riot of ghosts evaporating from the skin
of dead Mexicans who staggered for days without water through the desert.

Thirty years ago, a girl from the land of Zapata kissed me once
on the lips and died with my name nailed to hers like a broken door.
I kept a snapshot of the wedding; yesterday it washed ashore on my desk.

There was a conspiracy to commit a crime. This is my confession: I'd do it again.

Mr. and Mrs. Rodríguez Have Been Deported, Leaving Six Children Behind with the Neighbors

Please donate shoes
to this family
care of the Mesilla Cultural Center.

Rodríguez family shoe sizes:

Marina, age 17: size 6
Rocío, age 15: size 5
Memo, age 13: size 7
Jesús, age 12: size 7
José, age 8: size 4
Ana, age 5: size 3

The Rowboat

Twenty thousand years ago, the Mombacho volcano behind me blew its top, and half of it landed here in Lake Cocibolca, creating 365 islands—bad news for the volcano, great news for real estate investment, because you can buy one of these islands for your very own island paradise, and build on it.

—Howard Stableford, Home: World Nicaragua

The beggars cannot swim to the private islands of Lake Cocibolca. Instead they wander through the plaza in Granada, trailing after the investors in paradise who climb the steps of the cathedral to point cameras, light candles for the dead and ask forgiveness. In slavery days, an army of sunburned mercenaries paraded into the plaza. Their general proclaimed himself *The Gray-Eyed Man of Destiny*, then President of Nicaragua, English the language of the land and slavery the law. When the mercenaries fled Granada, looted brandy on their breath, a pestilence of flame crumbled the city's face. In Honduras, The Man of Destiny posed for the firing squad, and there was thunder in his skull like Mombacho raining islands on the lake.

On the private islands of Lake Cocibolca, there are stone walls and towers, picnic tables and gazebos, barbeques and swimming pools. The investors wave from hammocks, waiting for the mangos to drop and roll at their feet. In speedboats the masters of the lake explore the islands where the monkeys bellow in the trees. A blonde girl shares a bag of cashews with a white-bearded capuchin descending delicately from a branch over the boat. They squabble, shriek in each other's faces, and a shower of cashews spurts in the air as the gasoline engine snarls a getaway. The herons tiptoe quickly in the shallows, far from the bickering primates.

In the morning, at the hour called *la madrugada*, a rowboat circumnavigates the private islands of Lake Cocibolca. Boys and girls in blue and white uniforms huddle with their backpacks in the creaking boat, on their way to school again. The winds from the east swell and roll the muscles below the skin of the water;

the bull sharks wait in darkness for a body to tumble from the heaving deck.
The tallest girl rows, dipping one oar, then the other, leaning into the lake
as her brothers and sisters watch her without a word, or a shriek, or a song.
She is ten years old. She has rowed this archipelago for a thousand years.
This morning she must work the oars; tonight she will dream of firing squads.

The Swimming Pool at Villa Grimaldi

Santiago, Chile

Beyond the gate where the convoys spilled their cargo
of blindfolded prisoners, and the cells too narrow to lie down,
and the rooms where electricity convulsed the body
strapped across the grill until the bones would break,
and the parking lot where interrogators rolled pickup trucks
over the legs of subversives who would not talk,
and the tower where the condemned listened through the wall
for the song of another inmate on the morning of execution,
there is a swimming pool at Villa Grimaldi.

Here the guards and officers would gather families
for barbeques. The interrogator coached his son:
Kick your feet. Turn your head to breathe.
The torturer's hands braced the belly of his daughter,
learning to float, flailing at her lesson.

Here the splash of children, eyes red
from too much chlorine, would rise to reach
the inmates in the tower. The secret police
paraded women from the cells at poolside,
saying to them: *Dance for me.* Here the host
served chocolate cookies and Coke on ice
to the prisoner who let the names of comrades
bleed down his chin, and the prisoner
who refused to speak a word stopped breathing
in the water, facedown at the end of a rope.

When a dissident pulled by the hair from a vat
of urine and feces cried out for God, and the cry
pelted the leaves, the swimmers plunged below the surface,
touching the bottom of a soundless blue world.
From the ladder at the edge of the pool they could watch
the prisoners marching blindfolded across the landscape,
one hand on the shoulder of the next, on their way
to the afternoon meal and back again. The neighbors
hung bedsheets on the windows to keep the ghosts away.

There is a swimming pool at the heart of Villa Grimaldi,
white steps, white tiles, where human beings
would dive and paddle till what was human in them
had dissolved forever, vanished like the prisoners
thrown from helicopters into the ocean by the secret police,
their bellies slit so the bodies could not float.

The Buried Book of Jorge Montealegre

Santiago, Chile

Montealegre, Montealegre: another name on the list of subversives.
The soldiers burned his books and made him watch. At Chacabuco,
the prison camp in a desert of abandoned salt mines where rain
never spatters the dust, Montealegre kept a box of books
the other inmates called *the library*, guarding the rectangle
of cardboard as if a fallen bird struggled to breathe inside.
Montealegre wrote his first poem in a cell without light,
in a land without rain. The other inmates gave him
a diploma and a can of coffee for his adolescent verses.

Montealegre, Montealegre: exiled to Rome, where the fires of Chile
glimmered in his sleep. In his country everything was gone to smoke,
the books and the bodies of the disappeared, so Montealegre
turned to smoke, coming home unseen through ports and desert sky.
In Santiago, a compañero smuggled him the book of poems
the poet typed at night in the city of exile but had never seen,
the name *Montealegre* on the cover, pages flapping and trembling
in his hands for the first time, the bird in the box still alive.
A group forbidden to gather by the dictator gathered at the chapel
to hear the poet chant his songs of Chacabuco, land without rain.

Montealegre, Montealegre: the poet read the poems,
and the clouds scattered drops clear and fat in the desert
far away, the first rain in a hundred years. Montealegre
wandered through the incandescent desert of the book
till someone tugged his sleeve to stop his tongue.

Montealegre, stop, someone said. *I've read too long,*
he thought, but he was wrong. The police crept in a circle
around them, carabineros rapping at the chapel door.

Montealegre, Montealegre: the fire in his dreams came back again,
burning in the garden behind the chapel. Hurried hands
flung documents of incrimination: names, addresses, numbers.
Montealegre saw his name accusing him in black letters
on the cover of the book. He tore the cover off and watched
the paper shrivel in the flames, but could not bring himself to burn the book,
to make a burnt offering of this creature with a heartbeat, the words
with wings that would combust in hellish air. Montealegre buried
his only book, clawing at the earth, then walked out the chapel door,
hands above his head, knees damp with mud, to face the carabineros.

Montealegre, Montealegre: the name means *Joyful Mountain.*
The dictator was indicted for crimes against humanity and stiffened
in a stroke when he heard the news. Montealegre's black beard
is turning gray; he is standing by the window with a cup of black coffee.
Tomorrow or a hundred years from now the chief of police
could pass out a truckload of shovels, and the carabineros
could dig all night in the garden behind the chapel,
gouge a thousand holes in the ground, and never find the book.

Montealegre, Montealegre: he will not dig up the book. He would
tell you that the poems came from the dust of the desert, and have
returned to dust. He is the rain that fell on fire in Chile. In a land
of burning books, Jorge Montealegre saved a book from burning.

Part Two

BLASPHEMY

The *Playboy* Calendar and the
Rubáiyát of Omar Khayyám

The year I graduated from high school,
my father gave me a *Playboy* calendar
and the *Rubáiyát* of Omar Khayyám.
On the calendar, he wrote:
Enjoy the scenery.
In the book of poems, he wrote:
I introduce you to an old friend.

The Beast was my only friend in high school,
a wrestler who crushed the coach's nose with his elbow,
fractured the fingers of all his teammates,
could drink half a dozen vanilla milkshakes,
and signed up with the Marines
because his father was a Marine.
I showed the *Playboy* calendar to The Beast
and he howled like a silverback gorilla
trying to impress an expedition of anthropologists.
I howled too, smitten with the blonde
called *Miss January*, held high in my simian hand.

Yet, alone at night, I memorized the poet-astronomer
of Persia, his saints and sages bickering about eternity,
his angel looming in the tavern door with a jug of wine,
his *battered caravanserai* of sultans fading into the dark.
At seventeen, the laws of privacy have been revoked
by the authorities, and the secret police are everywhere:

I learned to hide Khayyám and his beard
inside the folds of the *Playboy* calendar
in case anyone opened the door without knocking,
my brother with a baseball mitt or a beery Beast.

I last saw The Beast that summer at the Marine base
in Virginia called Quantico. He rubbed his shaven head,
and the sunburn made the stitches from the car crash years ago
stand out like tiny crosses in the field of his face.
I last saw the *Playboy* calendar in December of that year,
when it could no longer tell me the week or the month.

I last saw Omar Khayyám this morning:
Awake! He said. *For Morning in the Bowl of Night
Has flung the Stone that puts the Stars to Flight.*

Awake! He said. And I awoke.

Blasphemy

for Sam Hamill

Let the blasphemy be spoken: poetry can save us,
not the way a fisherman pulls the drowning swimmer
into his boat, not the way Jesus, between screams,
promised life everlasting to the thief crucified beside him
on the hill, but salvation nevertheless.

Somewhere a convict sobs into a book of poems
from the prison library, and I know why
his hands are careful not to break the brittle pages.

Epiphany

for Adrian Mitchell (1932–2008)

Epiphany is not a blazing light. A blazing light
blazes when warplanes spread their demon's wings
and drop their demon's eggs over the city,
and the city burns like the eye of a screaming horse.

Epiphany is a comic book during the war.
A sailor on the convoy from New York to London
brought home bundles of American comics
that you studied like the scrolls of a world beyond the sun.
These were heroes who would never become a hand
waving goodbye from a pyramid of bricks.
The pages rolled: *Batman. Superman. Whit-Man.*

Walt Whit-Man. Whit-Man could not fly, yet he soared over mountains,
seeing the fur trapper and his native bride, the panther pacing in the branches.
He did not brawl with grinning villains, yet he was *one of the roughs,*
yanking doors off hinges, shouting about *the rights of them the others are down upon,*
as the auctioneer of shackled men and women cowered in his shadow.
He was far across the sea, yet he was there at the war hospital
unraveling the bandages, sponging clean the stump of an arm.
Whit-Man was a shape-shifter with a wizard's beard:
now the sailor in the crow's nest, now the mutineer in jail,
now the runaway slave leaning on a fencepost, out of breath.
He spoke in a tongue called *barbaric yawp*, mesmerized
by a spear of grass, amazed at the machinery of a mouse.

Epiphany is not a blazing light. Epiphany is a boy asking: *Is Whit-Man real?*
Epiphany is the poem you wrote in a boy's hand, the letters standing on shaky legs.
Epiphany is the poem you wrote to praise the great bell in the great singer's chest.
Epiphany is the poem you splattered against the windows of cathedrals.
Epiphany is the poem you raised your head to sing against the blazing light
of bombardment, as city after city burned like the eye of a screaming horse.
Epiphany is the night you sat in jail for trespass at the gates of the naval base
and the cop who called you *sir*, listening to every word about the missiles.
Epiphany is your creature the *Ape-Man* howling his poems in the forest,
even after the other creatures told him that howling would never change the forest.
Epiphany is the chorus of rebels, beggars, lunatics bellowing with your voice,
the flickering revelation that the words of the song in my head are your words.

Like a Word That Somersaults Through the Air

for Abe Osheroff (1915–2008)

His life begins with the rain, and the soggy cushions
of a couch left by the landlord to die on a Brooklyn sidewalk
in the year 1930. His life begins at age fifteen, Abe
the high school wrestler straining the cords in his neck

to lift the couch with the other boys back through the doorway
of a tenement in Brownsville. His life begins with a woman
who could not pay the rent staring dumbstruck on the corner
at the miracle of eviction evicted, the landlord a lord no more,

her sons and daughters trailing in a procession after the sofa.
His life begins with the cop who arrives on the corner
waving a revolver, the gun Abe snatches away to toss
across the pavement, squinting into the face of his first arrest.

His life begins with a cop's revolver bouncing off the asphalt,
like a word that somersaults through the air and cannot be unsaid.

How to Read Ezra Pound

At the poets' panel,
after an hour of poets
debating Ezra Pound,
Abe the Lincoln veteran,
remembering
the Spanish Civil War,
raised his hand and said:
If I knew
that a fascist
was a great poet,
I'd shoot him
anyway.

Walking

for Howard Zinn (1922–2010)

> *I go two steps closer, she moves two steps away. I walk ten steps and the horizon runs*
> *ten steps ahead. No matter how much I walk, I'll never reach her. What good is utopia?*
> *That's what: it's good for walking.*   —*Eduardo Galeano*

You walked alone, away from the city writhing in flames and jellied gasoline,

away from the canisters of napalm dropped by your bombardier's hands,

away from medals and ribbons stuffed in a folder with the words *never again*;

walking the backroads in a country of Confederate flags, shoes baked in mud,

shuffling on the picket line with dark-skinned sharecroppers, teachers, organizers

who hungered for the ballot box and sang all night to keep their jailers awake;

walking with apparitions, the escaped slave reading the compass of the moon

between the trees, the anarchist in spectacles who made of the crowd a roaring sea,

the union man on trial for subversion of the draft, who confessed the crime

and told the judge with open hands: *while there is a soul in prison, I am not free*;

walking through the metal detectors of courthouses and airports, smuggling

manifestos in your head from the slave, the anarchist, the unionist, words freed

as a magician frees doves flown to the rafters from the great stage of the world;

walking through schoolrooms, the smooth oval of faces tilted up, astonished

by your words as they floated down like parachutes of milkweed on the wind;

walking by the river with the fugitive poet-priest who sang of *the risen bread*,

as agents of the government hunted for the poet everywhere but the river;

walking through the mace that hissed in your eyes at the march against the war,

the cuffs that clicked, the billyclubs that jabbed the ribs of your thin body;

walking in the circle of the peace vigil on the town common at noon,

past the jeers and staring of the onlookers who know that nothing changes;

walking when your legs trembled in the storm of nerves crushed by the spine,

when you knew you would never arrive, that the world was too bright with ice

for a fistful of sand and careful steps, and yet your fingers still tapped out the messages of dissidents as you spoke, darting with the delirium of sparrows, walking with thousands beside you now, a roaring sea, down the road to a city where they greet you with blackberries that grow wild in the ruins, where scars of liquid fire dissolve into the skin, where the bombs will never fall again.

Visions of the Chapel Ceiling in Guadalajara

for Sandy Taylor (1931–2007) and Curbstone Press

Sandy, if you heard me, if you hear me:
I don't know why I said the words in Spanish.

I hated the words I heard on the phone—
stroke, coma, come now if you want to say goodbye—
turning like carousel horses in my head
as I drifted to the car, somehow forgetting
the book of poems to read at your bedside.
I hated the words I stuttered half-remembered
all the way to the hospital, the breath of my poems
sticking white as moths to the windshield.
I hated the words of the nurse who swore
I've seen them come back after the Last Rites,
then disappeared as if she did not mean it.

You had no words to say, you who would declaim *Ozymandias*
from memory, conjuring the wreckage of the pharaoh in the sand:
Look on my works, ye Mighty, and despair!
Now you snarled into the oxygen mask, refusing to die,
the gray radical who kept a shotgun in the corner for the Klan.
The missile strike that lit up the battlefield of your brain cheated us all.
If you had an hour before the firing squad, the poet in you
would have composed a last will and testament in rhyming couplets.

The nurse had left the room and we were alone that night
when the poems came back to me, the poems you always
asked me to read aloud, transmuted into books by the alchemy

of your printing press, and I who never learned to sing
could only drop the words like medicine in your ear:
En Jayuya,
los lagartijos se dispersan
como una flota de canoas verdes
ante el invasor.
In Jayuya,
the lizards scatter
like a fleet of green canoes
before the invader.

I don't know why I said the words in Spanish. I remembered
standing by your elbow to translate for you in Guadalajara,
where you wheeled a hand truck of books and baffled everyone
with the hopping three-legged dog of your accent.
Yet you knew the poets of our América,
their voices bursting like a thousand grackles
from the doors and windows of your house.
The rebel poet of El Salvador, who escaped his executioners
when the earthquake made of his jail an ancient ruin,
sits in your kitchen with coffee and bread, waiting for you.

You knew the way in Guadalajara, the orphanage,
the chapel at the orphanage, Orozco's murals at the chapel.
There were benches wide enough for lying down
to witness the visions on the ceiling: *El Hombre de Fuego,*
The Man of Fire, a being of flame walking on air,
soaring over the exhausted ashen creatures at his feet,
the stampede of conquistadores and priests,
the Indios writhing in their wake.

We had no need of words that day, two poets
silenced at last by the scratching of a paintbrush.
May you have visions of the chapel ceiling in Guadalajara.
May you meet *The Man of Fire* and shake his hand.
May you ignite a cigarette with his index finger.
May you cackle and cackle at your own joke.

The Day We Buried You in the Park

for Sandy Taylor

If you want me again look for me under your bootsoles.
                                   —Walt Whitman

The day we buried you in the park
I couldn't say no. Your wife had a plan,
revealed on the phone with the hush of conspiracy;
there are laws in this city against the interment
of human remains in public spaces.

This was the Poets' Park, your vision
floating like the black butterflies of cinders
over the house in ruins across the street.
You and Juan saw the stone steps flowing down
into the circle where the poets would stand and sing one day.
You and Juan saw the poets showering the air with words
and the trees drinking words like water.
You nailed up the sign and spread your arms to greet us
at the ceremony. This could not be explained
to the clerk who stamps the licenses
for the burial of the dead.

Juan began to cry when he saw your ashes
in the wheelbarrow. I shook him by the shoulder;
the neighbor who watches the park from her window
was eyeing us. I handed him the shovel.
We had to clamp our jaws like mobsters
stoically soiling their hands with the grit of a rival thug.

Your wife poured a bag of plant food over your ashes
in case the neighbor peeked too long through the hedges
or the cops rolled their cruiser to a stop, bored
after years of shoving drunks into the backseat.
We stirred the ashes with our hands till they turned white at the wrist,
and what I'd heard was true: there is bone that will not burn,
bodies that refuse to become dust, the stubborn shards of a man.
Ask any criminal who labors to bury the evidence.

We weren't criminals. We dug the hole in the wrong place,
ripped out the roots, grunted with every shovel full of rocks.
We made the little grave too big, then tossed away the dirt,
forgetting that we'd need to fill the hole once we dumped you in it.
When I tipped the wheelbarrow, your ashes landed with a puff,
drifting in the briefest of clouds over the grass, and Juan
dropped to his knees, crying again, giving us away.
The neighbor poked her head from the window
like a chicken suspicious of the world beyond the coop.

An hour after we began, I wore a mask of ash and sweat, black shoes white,
like the last man in the village to hear the warning of volcano,
or a miner on the first day back at work after the strike is lost,
or a believer smeared with his ancestors about to wash in the great river.
A woman who recognized my face stopped me as I crossed the street.
Did you just bury something in the park? she asked.
Why would I do a thing like that? I said.

The day we buried you in the park, I drove home
with three scoops of your ashes in a coffee can:

Chock full o'Nuts, the Heavenly Coffee, their slogan
emblazoned in a cloud across the New York skyline.
At your desk there was bad coffee and good poetry,
but no heaven, so I will look for you under my bootsoles,
walking through the world, soaking up the ghosts wherever I may go.

Instructions on the Disposal of My Remains

for Rich Villar and Fish Vargas

Don't scatter my ashes in the mountains or the ocean,
or the canals of a medieval city I always wanted to see,
or at the schoolyard in Brooklyn where I would run the bases.
Don't bury my body in the village of my ancestors,
or in a marble tomb surrounded by trees, where the poets
who make a pilgrimage to see me can carve their initials.

I want to be stuffed and mounted at the White Castle
in East Harlem. I want to welcome everyone, with glass eyes
and cotton in my head, to buy tiny steam-grilled burgers by the sack.
I want to stand in the doorway like a grizzly bear
at the Museum of Natural History, his mouth frozen
in a roar for all eternity, as if to tell the world:
That imperialist bastard Teddy Roosevelt shot me.

Once, in Mesilla, New Mexico, I saw a dummy of Billy the Kid
in a glass case. Put a quarter in the slot, the tape said,
and Billy the Kid will tell you the story of his escape
from the jailhouse that once stood on the site of this gift shop.

For a quarter, my cadaver, a miracle of taxidermy, would speak
in an almost-human voice of my first time at White Castle,
when I met a man at 4 AM who said he was a pirate,
and had the eyepatch to prove it. *I've lost my treasure map,*
he said. *Buy me a burger with onions, and I'll let you peek
under my eyepatch.* Under the patch, there was no eyeball.

This is why I want to be stuffed and mounted at White Castle.
Tell the faces at the window: Come to my wake, drop a quarter
in the slot, pose for snapshots grinning into your cell phone.
Buy the burgers by the sack till the day your heart explodes,
like a ketchup packet squashed on the floor of White Castle.
Join me in the ranks of the pirates and grizzly bears, roaring and lonely.

Litany at the Tomb of Frederick Douglass

Mount Hope Cemetery, Rochester, New York
November 7, 2008

This is the longitude and latitude of the impossible;

this is the epicenter of the unthinkable;

this is the crossroads of the unimaginable:

the tomb of Frederick Douglass, three days after the election.

This is a world spinning away from the gravity of centuries,

where the grave of a fugitive slave has become an altar.

This is the tomb of a man born as chattel, who taught himself to read in secret,

scraping the letters in his name with chalk on wood; now on the anvil-flat stone

a campaign button fills the O in *Douglass*. The button says: *Obama*.

This is the tomb of a man in chains, who left his fingerprints

on the slavebreaker's throat so the whip would never carve his back again;

now a labor union T-shirt drapes itself across the stone, offered up

by a nurse, a janitor, a bus driver. A sticker on the sleeve says: *I Voted Today.*

This is the tomb of a man who rolled his call to arms off the press,

peering through spectacles at the abolitionist headline; now a newspaper

spreads above his dates of birth and death. The headline says: *Obama Wins.*

This is the stillness at the heart of the storm that began in the body

of the first slave, dragged aboard the first ship to America. Yellow leaves

descend in waves, and the newspaper flutters on the tomb, like the sails

Douglass saw in the bay, like the eyes of a slave closing to watch himself

escape with the tide. Believers in spirits would see the pages trembling

on the stone and say: *look how the slave boy teaches himself to read.*

I say a prayer, the first in years: that here we bury what we call

the impossible, the unthinkable, the unimaginable, now and forever. *Amen.*

NOTES ON THE POEMS

The Trouble Ball: Satchel Paige, considered by many to be the greatest pitcher in the history of baseball, was excluded from the major leagues until 1948 due to a policy of racial segregation. He did, however, pitch throughout Latin America, including Puerto Rico, where he played for the Guayama Brujos (Witches or Sorcerers) in the 1939–40 and 1940–41 seasons. Stanza two relies in part on *Satchel: The Life and Times of an American Legend* (Random House, 2009) by Larry Tye. The poem is also based on a series of e-mail interviews with my father, Frank Espada, in November 2009. In Spanish and Latin American tradition, "Baltasar" was the king from Africa who, with two other kings, brought gifts to the infant Jesus; his image appears throughout Puerto Rico.

Blessed Be the Truth-Tellers: Jack Agüeros is a poet, fiction writer, translator, activist, and former director of El Museo del Barrio. Agüeros is now suffering from Alzheimer's disease; a benefit to defray his medical expenses was held at the Julia de Burgos Cultural Arts Center in East Harlem in March 2008. This poem was written for the occasion. "Ay bendito," which literally means, "Oh, blessed," is a common Puerto Rican expression of empathy, pity, or dismay, roughly equivalent to the Yiddish "oy vey." "Cuchifrito" is a term applied to a variety of Puerto Rican fried foods.

People Like Us Are Dangerous: Carlos Ortiz, from Ponce, Puerto Rico, was two-time lightweight boxing champion of the world between 1962 and 1968. Ortiz defended his title against Ismael Laguna of Colón, Panamá, by fifteen-round decision in August 1967 at Shea Stadium in New York. The description of the bout relies in part on contemporary newspaper accounts and a chapter in *The Hardest Game: McIlvanney on Boxing* (McGraw-Hill, 2001) by Hugh McIlvanney. Ortiz and Laguna have both been inducted into the International Boxing Hall of Fame. Laguna's nickname—"El Tigre," or the Tiger of San Lorenzo—refers to the district of Colón where he was born.

A Traveling Salesman in the Gardens of Paradise: There is a public housing project called "Jardines del Paraíso," or the Gardens of Paradise, in Río Piedras, outside San Juan, Puerto Rico. My grandmother lived there for many years. "Arroz con pollo" is chicken with rice; a "tecato" is a junkie.

Isabel's Corrido: A corrido is a traditional Mexican narrative song form, addressing subjects that range from tragic love to revolutionary history. "The land of Zapata" refers to Emiliano Zapata, famed leader of the 1910 Mexican Revolution, and the state of Morelos in México, where he—and Isabel—were born. "Quiero ver las fotos" means, "I want to see the photos."

Mr. and Mrs. Rodríguez Have Been Deported, Leaving Six Children Behind with the Neighbors: This poem is based on an item in an e-mail newsletter from Denise Chávez and the Mesilla Cultural Center in Mesilla, New Mexico.

The Rowboat: "The Gray-Eyed Man of Destiny" was William Walker, a "filibuster" or privateer from Nashville, Tennessee, who invaded Granada, Nicaragua, with a mercenary army in 1855, declared himself president of Nicaragua in 1856, was forced to flee, and was finally executed in Honduras in 1860. The first stanza relies in part on *Under the Big Stick: Nicaragua and the United States Since 1848* (South End Press, 1986) by Karl Bermann. The poem is based on a visit to Granada and Lake Cocibolca, also known as Lake Nicaragua, in February 2006. "La madrugada," in the third stanza, refers to daybreak or early morning. The epigraph is a direct quote from a promotional video for an international real estate agency.

The Swimming Pool at Villa Grimaldi: Villa Grimaldi was a center of interrogation, torture, and execution in Santiago, Chile, during the dictatorship of General Augusto Pinochet. The poem is based on a visit to the Villa Grimaldi site—now converted into a peace park—in the company of my Chilean translator, Oscar Sarmiento, in March 2007. Part of the original Villa Grimaldi structure is a swimming pool used by the guards, police officers, and their families. The poem relies in part on "The Ethnography of Villa Grimaldi in Pinochet's Chile: From Public Landscape to Secret Detention Centre (1973–1980)" (Latin American Studies Association Papers, 2003) by Mario Aguilar; *Battling for Hearts and Minds: Memory Struggles in Pinochet's Chile, 1973–1988* (Duke University Press, 2006) by Steve Stern; *The Inferno: A Story of Terror and Survival in Chile* (University of Wisconsin Press, 2004) by Luz Arce; and *Parque por la Paz Villa Grimaldi: una deuda con nosotros mismos,* published by Chile's Ministerio de Vivienda y Urbanismo in 1997. A conversation with Steve Stern, a professor and mentor of mine at the University of Wisconsin–Madison thirty years ago, was essential to the poem.

The Buried Book of Jorge Montealegre: A poet and journalist born in Santiago, Chile, in 1954, Jorge Montealegre Iturra was arrested and incarcerated in the National Stadium with thousands of others following the military coup on September 11, 1973. Two months later, he was shipped to the Chacabuco prison camp in the Atacama desert of northern Chile. In exile, he wrote an account of his experience called *Chacabuco* (1975) and his first book of poems, *Huiros,* or *Seaweed* (1979), published in Paris the same year he returned to Chile. He received a Guggenheim Fellowship in 1989. Montealegre is also the former director of the Consejo de Fomento del Libro y la Lectura, or the Council for the Promotion of Books and Reading in Chile. This poem is based on a conversation with Montealegre in Santiago, Chile, in March 2007. The poem also relies in part on an interview by Alejandro Lavquen with Montealegre in *Punto Final* (August 29, 2003), and an article entitled, "Film to be Made in Chile About Pinochet-Era Prison Camp" by Niles Atallah from the *Santiago Times*, May 6, 2006.

The *Playboy* Calendar and the *Rubáiyát* of Omar Khayyám: "Awake! for Morning in the Bowl of Night / Has flung the Stone that puts the Stars to Flight . . ." The fifth stanza quotes the first two lines from the *Rubáiyát* of Omar Khayyám, in the 1859 translation by Edward FitzGerald. The phrase "battered caravanserai" also comes from this translation.

Blasphemy: Sam Hamill, to whom the poem is dedicated, is a poet, translator, essayist, editor, and activist. He founded both Copper Canyon Press and Poets Against War.

Epiphany: "the rights of them the others are down upon . . ." Stanza three quotes, paraphrases, and alludes to Walt Whitman's "Song of Myself" (especially #10, #24, and #33), "I Sing the Body Electric," and "The Wound-Dresser." Adrian Mitchell was a poet, translator, dramatist, and pacifist, proclaimed the "Shadow Poet Laureate" of the U.K. In December 2006, Mitchell was arrested and jailed for his part in a protest against the presence of the Trident nuclear submarine at a naval base in Faslane, Scotland. He was seventy-four years old at the time of his arrest. "[T]he poem you raised your head to sing against the blazing light / of bombardment" refers to Mitchell's antiwar anthem, "To Whom It May Concern." The "Ape-Man" is a character of Mitchell's invention. "[T]he chorus of rebels, beggars, lunatics bellowing with your voice" refers to Mitchell's English translation of the lyrics and other verses in the play *Marat/Sade* by Peter Weiss.

Like a Word That Somersaults Through the Air: Abe Osheroff was a political activist for nearly eighty years, from the age of fifteen till his death at the age of ninety-two. His activism began with the anti-eviction movement of the 1930s in Brooklyn, New York.

How to Read Ezra Pound: Osheroff was a veteran of the Abraham Lincoln Brigade, the American volunteers who fought against fascist forces in the Spanish Civil War (1936–1939). He made this comment on Pound (and the poet's fascist views) at a summer writers' conference held by the William Joiner Center for the Study of War and Social Consequences at the University of Massachusetts-Boston.

Walking: "I go two steps closer, she moves two steps away . . ." The epigraph by Eduardo Galeano comes from "Window on Utopia" and his book, *Walking Words* (W. W. Norton, 1995). Howard Zinn was a historian, teacher, and political activist. His landmark work, *A People's History of the United States* (HarperCollins, 1980) has sold more than two million copies to date. The poem relies in part for biographical information on Zinn's autobiography, *You Can't Be Neutral on a Moving Train* (Beacon Press, 1994). The "city writhing in flames and jellied gasoline" is Royan in France, bombed by the Allies in 1945. Zinn was a U.S. Air Force bombardier who flew a mission over Royan, then renounced his actions and war itself. "[S]huffling on the picket line" refers to Zinn's experience with the civil rights movement in Hattiesburg, Mississippi, and elsewhere. The "anarchist in spectacles who made of the crowd a roaring sea" is Emma Goldman; Zinn wrote a play about Goldman, called *Emma* (South End Press, 2002). The "union man" is socialist Eugene V. Debs; he made the statement, "While there is a soul in prison, I am not free" as part of his address to the court after being convicted in 1919 of violating the Espionage Act for opposing the draft during World War I. The "fugitive poet-priest" is Daniel Berrigan, one of the "Catonsville Nine" sought by the FBI after being convicted and sentenced for burning draft records in Catonsville, Maryland, during the Vietnam War. "[T]he risen bread" is a quotation from one of Berrigan's poems, "To the New York West Side Jesuit Community," and provides the title of his collection, *And the Risen Bread: Selected Poems 1957–1997* (Fordham University Press, 1998). "[T]he mace that hissed in your eyes at the march against the war" refers to an encounter between Zinn, Daniel Ellsberg, and police that occurred at a demonstration in Washington, D.C., in 1971.

Visions of the Chapel Ceiling in Guadalajara: "Look on my works, ye Mighty, and despair!" Stanza three quotes the poem "Ozymandias" by Percy Bysshe Shelley, as recited by Alexander "Sandy" Taylor. Taylor was a poet, translator, editor and cofounder of Curbstone Press, which published many leading Latino and Latin American writers over three decades, often in bilingual editions. Stanza four quotes my own poem, "Colibrí," in English and Spanish, from *Rebellion Is the Circle of a Lover's Hands,* published by Taylor and Curbstone in 1990; Jayuya is a town in the central mountains of Puerto Rico. In stanza five, "the rebel poet of El Salvador" refers to Roque Dalton, also published by Taylor and Curbstone. Stanza six refers to José Clemente Orozco, the great Mexican muralist, and his fresco called "El Hombre de Fuego" ("The Man of Fire") at the Hospicio Cabañas in Guadalajara, México.

The Day We Buried You in the Park: "If you want me again look for me under your bootsoles . . ." The epigraph comes from "Song of Myself" (#52) by Walt Whitman.

Litany at the Tomb of Frederick Douglass: This poem is based on a visit to the tomb of Frederick Douglass in Rochester, New York, immediately after the election of President Barack Obama in November 2008. The poem also refers to several incidents in the autobiographical *Narrative of the Life of Frederick Douglass, an American Slave, Written by Himself* (W. W. Norton, 1996).

Biographical Note

Called "the Latino poet of his generation" and "the Pablo Neruda of North American authors," Martín Espada was born in Brooklyn, New York, in 1957. He has published more than fifteen books as a poet, editor, essayist, and translator, including two collections of poems in 2008: *Crucifixion in the Plaza de Armas* (Smokestack, 2008), released in England, and *La Tumba de Buenaventura Roig* (Terranova, 2008), a bilingual edition published in Puerto Rico. *The Republic of Poetry*, a collection of poems published by W. W. Norton in 2006, received the Paterson Award for Sustained Literary Achievement and was a finalist for the Pulitzer Prize. Another collection, *Imagine the Angels of Bread* (W. W. Norton, 1996), won an American Book Award and was a finalist for the National Book Critics Circle Award. Other books of poetry include *Alabanza: New and Selected Poems* (W. W. Norton, 2003), *A Mayan Astronomer in Hell's Kitchen* (W. W. Norton, 2000), *City of Coughing and Dead Radiators* (W. W. Norton, 1993), and *Rebellion Is the Circle of a Lover's Hands* (Curbstone, 1990). He has received numerous awards and fellowships, including the Robert Creeley Award, the Antonia Pantoja Award, the Charity Randall Citation, the Paterson Poetry Prize, the Gustavus Myers Outstanding Book Award, the National Hispanic Cultural Center Literary Award, the Premio Fronterizo, two NEA Fellowships, the PEN/Revson Fellowship, a USA Simon Fellowship, and a Guggenheim Foundation Fellowship. His poems have appeared in *The New Yorker*, *The New York Times Book Review*, *Harper's*, *The Nation*, and *The Best American Poetry*. He has also published two collection of essays, *The Lover of a Subversive Is Also a Subversive* (Michigan, 2010) and *Zapata's Disciple* (South End, 1998); edited two anthologies, *El Coro: A Chorus of Latino and Latina Poetry* (University of Massachusetts, 1997) and *Poetry Like Bread: Poets of the Political Imagination from Curbstone Press* (Curbstone, 1994); and released an audiobook of poetry called *Now the Dead Will Dance the Mambo* (Leapfrog, 2004). His work has been translated into ten languages. A former tenant lawyer, Espada is now a professor in the Department of English at the University of Massachusetts-Amherst, where he teaches creative writing and the work of Pablo Neruda.